From Me To YouTube: The Unofficial Guide To Bethany Mota

by Emily Klein

Scholastic Inc.

Photos ©: cover: George Pimentel/Getty Images; back cover top: Imeh Akpanudosen/Getty Images; back cover bottom left: Noel Vasquez/Getty Images; back cover bottom right: Kevin Winter/SAs 2014 /Getty Images; 4: Dan Steinberg/Invision/AP Images; 7: Jaguar PS/Shutterstock, Inc.; 9: Noel Vasquez/Getty Images; 10: George Pimentel/Getty Images; 13: Barry King/FilmMagic/Getty Images; 14: Stephen Lovekin/FilmMagic/Getty Images; 17: Imeh Akpanudosen/Getty Images for ELLE; 19: Anthony Behar/AP Images; 20: Mike Coppola/Getty Images for Go Red; 23 top: FayesVision/WENN.com/Newscom; 23 bottom: Dimitrios Kambouris/Getty Images for YouTube; 25: Taylor Hill/Getty Images; 26 top: Timothy Hiatt/Getty Images for Aéropostale; 26 center: Laura Cavanaugh/FilmMagic/ Getty Images; 26 bottom: George Pimentel/Getty Images for Aéropostale; 29: Laura Cavanaugh/FilmMagic/Getty Images; 30: FayesVision/WENN.com/Alamy Images; 33 left, 33 right: George Pimentel/Getty Images for Aéropostale; 35: Timothy Hiatt/Getty Images for Aéropostale; 36: Adam Taylor/ABC via Getty Images; 39 top, bottom: Adam Taylor/ABC via Getty Images; 40: Michael Simon/startraksphoto.com; 43: Rommel Demano/Getty Images; 44: Jerod Harris/WireImage/ Getty Images; 44: Laura Cavanaugh/FilmMagic/Getty Images; 44: Kevin Winter/Getty Images; 46: George Pimentel/Getty Images for Aéropostale.

UNAUTHORIZED:
This book is not sponsored by or affiliated with Bethany Mota or anyone involved with her.

© 2015 by Scholastic

ISBN 978-0-545-87572-1

10 9 8 7 6 5 4 3 2 1   15 16 17 18 19

Printed in the U.S.A.   40
First printing 2015

Introduction

Imagine shooting to super-stardom just by doing your hobby. You'd have tons of fans, travel to the coolest places, and get to spin your dream career into reality. It would be awesome!

Bethany Mota had no idea she was sitting on the brink of fan-mania when she filmed her first YouTube video at thirteen years old. "I was really bored . . . It was the summertime. So what do you do when you're bored in the summertime? You watch YouTube videos," Bethany said in a *HuffPost Live* interview. Soon after, Bethany started filming her own vids from her bedroom. She'd talk about makeup, hair, or her latest fashion buys. And she'd hope someone would watch.

With time, Bethany's subscriber list grew . . . and grew . . . and grew—until it exploded. Today, she has millions of fans all over the world who call themselves "Motavators." She also has two super-popular YouTube channels, her own collections at the ever-trendy fashion store Aéropostale, a hit song, and she was the first YouTuber to compete on *Dancing with the Stars*. She has sparkled on the cover of some fab mags. And she got to interview President Obama!

But Bethany hasn't always lived this fairy tale. She suffered through cyber-bullying and was really down for a while. With YouTube, Bethany found her voice. Now she uses that voice to inspire others.

Chapter 1:
Baby Beth

Bethany Mota was born in California on November 7, 1995. Her parents' names are Tony and Tammy. Bethany also has a sister named Brittany who is five years older. Bethany has lots of fun childhood memories of her fam. They took trips to places like Disneyland. They also spent time with extended family. It was a good thing that the Motas were close because Bethany was a super-shy kid. She told *HuffPost Live*, "People thought I was mute . . . The only people who heard me talk were my parents and my sister."

Bethany's family moved to a small town called Los Banos when she was five. There, Bethany met her bestie, Alyssa. They'd have

sleepovers, watch scary movies, and make forts in the living room. Bethany was kind of a tomboy but she also loved playing with her dollhouse, obsessing over Neopets, and wearing her Rugrats bathing suit year round. When Bethany was little, she dreamed of becoming a fashion designer. "I would . . . pretend that all the clothes in my closet were designed by me . . ." she said in a *Yahoo Finance* video interview.

The Mota sisters were homeschooled when they were little. When Brittany decided that she wanted to go to public school, their mom sent both girls. Bethany was in the third grade.

At first, Bethany didn't have any friends. During recess, she'd stand alone in the school hallways singing Lizzie McGuire songs instead of playing outside with the other kids. Eventually, Bethany made two best buds, Emma and Cecilia. The three

girls did everything together. They dressed in the same outfits, and they wore purses instead of backpacks.

In sixth grade, Bethany didn't have any classes with Emma or Cecilia. This made her feel lonely. Bethany decided to try cheerleading after school. There, she met two new besties, Samrah and Savannah. They totally bonded. One of Bethany's best memories is when the three girls went to a Hannah Montana concert. Bethany was in fan-heaven!

Bethany was having loads of fun. But over the next few months, things began to change.

Chapter 2:
Bethany's Bully Story

*B*ethany enjoyed her winter break in sixth grade, but as vacay came to a close, she started getting anxious. She didn't want to be alone again at school. She was also extra sad because her grandpa passed away. She asked her mom if she could be homeschooled again. Her mom said okay.

After that, Bethany started even more activities. She enrolled in dance classes and performed in competitions. She started acting and singing classes. She even played an orphan in a local production of *Annie*. Bethany's life was going fab until someone at her old school started cyber-bullying her.

A girl who Bethany knew made a fake Myspace page and said mean things about her. She called Bethany fat and ugly. She also turned some of Bethany's old friends against her. "I thought that I could trust these people and they turned on me . . ." Bethany said in a *Dancing with the Stars* video interview. "I just felt that no one else knew what I was going through. I felt like I had lost my voice."

Bethany was crushed. She couldn't eat, so she started losing weight. And she was having anxiety attacks. Bethany stopped going to her classes and activities. Her confidence slipped away.

One day, she stumbled upon beauty videos on YouTube. They cheered her up. "I was actually not familiar with the beauty community at the time . . . I thought it was so cool," Bethany said in a *HuffPost Live* interview. Soon after, Bethany decided to record her own videos.

Chapter 3:
The Beginning of "Macbarbie07"

In June of 2009, Bethany filmed her first YouTube video. She practically whispered through it. She didn't want her family to know what she was doing. She thought they would make fun of her. "My first video was very embarrassing . . . I was so awkward and I was nervous because I didn't want anyone in my house to know that I was making videos," she told *HuffPost Live*. She named her channel "Macbarbie07" after the MAC makeup Barbie collection from 2007.

Bethany told her mom about her videos first. She asked her mom to buy makeup to talk about in her videos. Bethany's dad was super-confused when he saw makeup arriving at the house for his not-so-girly daughter.

Bethany decided to create "hauls"—or videos showing her purchases and reviews of the products. She also filmed hair and make-up how-tos. Her mom and sister weren't into beauty stuff. Bethany learned all her tips and tricks online.

Bethany didn't become a YouTube queen overnight. Her success took time. In the beginning, no one even watched her videos. Bethany thought about quitting.

Luckily, Bethany kept making videos. She found her voice again. And she got comfortable just being herself. Bethany grew into a YouTube sensation. She has come a long way since that sad, bullied girl. "Now I truly am confident in myself," Bethany said in a video clip from *Dancing with the Stars*. She added, "I wish that I could tell myself 'Look at what you're gonna be doing.'"

"Macbarbie07," now dubbed "Bethany

Mota," has since morphed into a lifestyle channel. Bethany still creates fashion, hair, and makeup tutorials. But according to her YouTube page, she also posts videos about DIY projects and anything else that she loves. In 2010, Bethany launched a second YouTube channel called "BethanysLife." This channel focuses more on her personal life.

23

Chapter 4:
YouTube Stardom

*T*oday, Bethany reigns over social media with over ten million subscribers between her two YouTube channels, more than two million Twitter followers, and just over four million followers on Instagram. In 2014, Bethany was the number-one-Googled fashion designer. Bethany Mota is officially epic.

"To get 100 subscribers was just mind-blowing to me," Bethany said in a *Yahoo Finance* video clip. She still remembers the first time a Motavator recognized her in the mall. ". . . I heard this girl calling my name . . . I'm like, 'Wait, I don't know this girl—what's going on?'" she said in an *Adweek* interview. Bethany loves meeting her fans in person. She said in that same interview, ". . . It's like, 'Wow,

there's actual real people who watch my videos.'"" It's her fans' support that keeps her going.

Bethany's popularity hasn't happened by accident. She works hard to create the perfect videos for her viewers. She'll sometimes get help shooting the vids, but she does the editing herself. The beauty and fashion videos can take four days to perfect. "I am also a slow editor, because I'll analyze every little detail . . ." she told *Refinery 29*.

As soon as she posts a video, Bethany checks the comments and responds. She also sends out tweets and posts on her other social media throughout the day. Bethany hearts her fans. And she'll always be there for them.

Even with all of her fame, Bethany still has some haters. And she has had to learn how to deal with them. Early on, Bethany started getting some hate-comments. She didn't understand how strangers could be so mean toward

her. She told *Business Insider*, "Some of them just want attention. You have to treat them nicely or don't respond at all."

One girl was especially negative. In the same *Business Insider* interview, Bethany shared that she messaged the girl and said, "I don't know why you don't like me." She went on to say, "I just wanted you to know that I don't have anything negative toward you and wish you nothing but the best." The message worked! The girl apologized. She then defended Bethany in the comments.

Bethany offers aspiring YouTubers this advice: "Upload as much as you can, but the interaction is so important, too. You need to build that relationship and friendship with your audience," she told *Refinery 29*. She added, "I always think about what I can create for my audience, not what they can do for me."

As for her own success, Bethany believes

that just being herself is most important. In a *MyFoxNY* interview she said, "With my YouTube videos I'm just being me."

Chapter 5: Red Carpets and More

*B*ethany gets opportunities that most girls only dream about. She's invited to celeb-packed red-carpet events. She wins high-profile awards. And she flies all over the world to meet her Motavators.

In 2014, *Entertainment Tonight* asked Bethany to interview celebs on the orange carpet for Nickelodeon's Kids' Choice Awards. She talked to stars like Bella Thorne, Zendaya, and Lea Michele. The stars dished with her on their pre-show beauty tips. That same year, she also went to the MTV Movie Awards!

Bethany doesn't always just "walk the carpet." In 2014, she won two awesome awards. She nabbed the Streamy Award for Best Fashion Channel, Show or Series, and won Choice

Web Star with Tyler Oakley at the Teen Choice Awards. Bethany also had a fangirl moment at the Teen Choice Awards. She snapped a selfie with Ansel Elgort from *The Fault in Our Stars*!

Another cool part of Bethany's life is traveling the world to talk about social media. She also sets up "meet-and-greets" with fans. Some of her international stops have been China, Singapore, India, and Australia. (She learned how to surf in Australia—so cool!) And everywhere she goes, Bethany's Motavators welcome her. While traveling in Japan, 800 fans met at a park when Bethany said she'd be there. "Everywhere I travel out of the country, it always blows my mind how many people actually know about my channel there," she said in an *LA Times* article.

Bethany also went on a Motavatour. She rode a tour bus to Aéropostales around the country to meet her fans. Bethany had the best time on her awesome bus. The outside had her pic and name on it. And the inside was fixed up like her bedroom at home—amaze!

Chapter 6:
Beyond YouTube

Bethany's YouTube domination has opened many doors. She rocked the cover of uber mags *Seventeen* and *Fast Company*. She guest-judged on *Project Runway*. And she's worked on projects with Forever 21 and JCPenney. A lot of brands ask Bethany to try their products. But Bethany is picky about saying yes. In a *MyFoxNY* interview, she said, "I really want my viewers to think they can trust me."

In December of 2013, Bethany's childhood dream came true when she debuted her very own clothing line at Aéropostale. First, the store tapped her to pick "Bethany's Faves" for their website. Next, they asked her to design her own Aero clothing collection. Bethany told *Business Insider* that she can choose the

colors, patterns, and how she wants it done. She explained, "They're very open to my ideas." Bethany has created bedding, jewelry, and even her own perfume for the store. (All adorbs, of course.) Bethany told *Adweek*, "Seeing my viewers wear . . . the things that I design, you never think that's going to happen."

Bethany also got to slip back into her dancing shoes when she competed on *Dancing with the Stars*. She partnered with Derek Hough on season 19. "I decided to do *Dancing with the Stars* because it absolutely terrified me," she said in a video clip from the show. Bethany was nervous about performing live. But she rose to the challenge.

The duo wowed audiences and moved the judges to tears with their dance about bullying. And Bethany got a shout-out from Taylor Swift after another performance. Tay tweeted that she liked Bethany's dance to her song, "Shake

It Off." Over the weeks, Bethany danced her way to the two-part finale. Bethany lost her chance at the Mirror Ball trophy in week eleven. But she kept moving.

Bethany's first single, "Need You Right Now" with fellow YouTuber Mike Tompkins, was released in October of 2014. With her Motavators' support (including cutie Kevin Jonas!), the song quickly shot to number three on iTunes. Fans also boosted the song up the Billboard and Twitter Real Time charts.

In January of 2015, Bethany was chosen, along with two other YouTubers, to interview President Obama. How cool! The two chatted about topics like bullying, why politics are important, and which superpowers they would want. And, of course, Bethany snapped a selfie with the prez.

Chapter 7:
Bethany @ Home

Even with all of her rad projects, Bethany still finds time to chill out. When she's not working, Bethany is like most girls her age. She watches YouTube videos and movies in bed. And she likes to sketch while listening to music. "It's also important to just sit in your room alone and relax," she said in a *Refinery 29* interview. Bethany likes to stay up late. But when she was on *Dancing with the Stars*, she'd be exhausted by ten at night.

Bethany told *Teen Vogue* that it's hard to fit exercise into her schedule. She'll go for a run or bike ride, do an exercise video, or just turn on some tunes and dance. If she gets to the gym, Bethany runs on the treadmill, cycles, and stretches.

Even though Bethany's crazy popular for her beauty channel, she's low-key with her own look. When she first started wearing makeup in sixth grade, she wore some powder, light gloss, and mascara. She'd buy lots of makeup. Now, she only buys something when she runs out of a product.

Today, her everyday look includes BB cream, under-eye concealer, a touch of powder, mascara, cream blush, and Maybelline Baby Lips lip balm. She also fills in her brows. When she goes out at night, Bethany may add some fun eye makeup. To complete her look, Bethany rocks beachy waves. She often braids her hair before bed so she can wake up with the perfect 'do.

As for her personal style, Bethany told *Business Insider*, "Definitely bohemian . . . It's also girly and very comfortable." She added, "Once in a while I can be a little edgy." Bethany

shops at fan-faves like Forever 21, Urban Outfitters, H&M, and Aéropostale (obvs).

So, what's coming next from this superstar? She's holding off on college so she can concentrate on work. Bethany told *Refinery 29*, "I just want to keep creating things. I love to think of things that haven't been done and then bring them to life . . ." And she'll be making vids as long as her fans want them. Bethany told the *LA Times*, "I feel that I was given this voice to use to speak to all these people around the world, so I want to make sure I use that the best and smartest way possible."

Fun Facts

Birthday: November 7, 1995

Hometown: Los Banos

Parents' Names: Tony and Tammy

Sibling: Brittany

Nationality: Portuguese

Nicknames: Beth, Bethers, Betherson, Bethels, Bether

Pet: Labradoodle named Winnie

Height: 5' 3 ¼"

Zodiac Sign: Scorpio

First Perfume Purchase: Hannah Montana

Favorite Quote: "Decide you want your dream more than it scares you."

Favorite Colors: turquoise, white, and gold

Fears: spiders, snakes, and being unhappy for a long time

Favorite Sweet Flavor: marshmallow

Favorite Piece of Jewelry: stackable rings

Favorite Animal: meerkat

Celebrity Style Inspirations: Lauren Conrad, Vanessa Hudgens, and Selena Gomez

Celebrity She Would Most Like to Style: Katy Perry

Favorite Cereal: Raisin Bran

Official Twitter: @BethanyMota

Official Instagram: @bethanynoelm

Official YouTube: youtube.com/Macbarbie07